FIGHTING FORCES OF WORLD WAR II

ON LAND

John C. Miles

CAPSTONE PRESS
a capstone imprint

Edge Books are published by Capstone Press
1710 Roe Crest Drive, North Mankato, Minnesota 56003
www.mycapstone.com

Library of Congress Cataloging-in-Publication Data
Library of Congress Cataloging-in-Publication data is available on the
Library of Congress website:

ISBN 978-1-5435-7483-8 (library binding)

Summary: Explores the military units that battled to control
precious territory in World War II, and provides information about key
battles, tactics, and weapons that helped propel the Allies to victory.

Editorial Credits
Editor: Julia Bird
Series designer: John Christopher/White Design
Photo researcher: Diana Morris

Photo Credits
Alchetron/CC Wikimedia Commons: 19t. BlankaB/Shutterstock: 14tl. Martin Brayley/
Dreamstime: 25c. Bundesarchiv photo/CC Wikimedia Commons: 9t. CBW/Alamy:
20b. Chronicle/Alamy: 8b, 21b, 25b. David Conway/Alamy: 13br. Sgt C J Dawson, No 2
Army Film & Photographic Unit/IWM: 17b. Reg J. Edwards/Australian War Memorial:
14b. Everett Collection/Alamy: 27c. Everett Historical/Shutterstock: front cover b, 4bl,
4tr, 5t, 9b, 19c. Fox Photos/Getty Images: 7b. Hulton Archive/Getty Images: 13t, 28c.
Hulton Deutsch/Getty Images: 6b. IWM: 13bl. Maj. Geoffrey Keating, No 1 Army Film
& Photographic Unit/IWM: 16b. Keystone France/Gamma Keystone/Getty Images: 21c.
Lt W T Lockeyear/IWM via Getty Images: 16c. Militarist/Shutterstock: 20tl. Military
Images/Alamy: 29t. Musée de L'Armée, Paris/Rama/CC Wikimedia Commons: 11b.
Muszeum Orla Bialego/CC Wikimedia Commons: 17c. National Library of Canada:
23b. Olemac/Shutterstock: 21t. Photo 12/Coll-DITE/USIA/Alamy: 22b. Photo 12/UIG/
Getty Images: 11t. Pictorial Parade/Getty Images: 18b. Popperfoto/Getty Images: 7tr,
12b. Print Collector/Getty Images: 7tl. Edward Reeves/Alamy: 15t. RLCM: 6tl. S-dmit/
Dreamstime: front cover t, back cover, 1. Trinity Mirror/Mirrorpix/Alamy: 15b, 26b.
Ullstein Bild/Getty Images: 5b, 19b. U.S. Army Photo: 24b, 27b. U.S. Army Photo/
CC Wikimedia Commons: 24tl, 26tl. U.S. Signal Corps photograph/CC Wikimedia
Commons: 23c. Vector Plotnikoff/Shutterstock: 18tl. WHA/Alamy: 10b, 27t.
CC Wikimedia Commons: 8tl, 10tl, 12tl, 16tl, 22tl, 28tl.

First published in Great Britain in 2018
by The Watts Publishing Group
Copyright © The Watts Publishing Group, 2018

Printed and bound in China
1593

Table of Contents

War Begins

In 1918 Germany lost World War I (1914–1918) and was forced to sign the Treaty of Versailles. Its harsh terms were very unpopular with Germans. In 1933 they elected a new leader, Adolf Hitler, who promised to restore Germany's standing in the world.

Hitler rides through cheering crowds in the German city of Kassel in 1939.

Rise of the Nazis

Hitler's Nazi (National Socialist) Party believed that their country should rule over all others and that certain groups of people, such as Jews, were trying to cheat Germany. Under the Nazis, Germany began to build up its armed forces and take over land in nearby countries. Finally, on September 1, 1939, German forces invaded neighboring Poland.

Allied Forces and Axis Powers

Great Britain, and the countries of its empire and dominions, joined France to declare war on Germany. These countries became known as the Allied forces. During 1940 Hitler took control of Denmark, Norway, France, Belgium, and the Netherlands. Italy joined the war on the side of the Nazis, forming the Axis powers. They were later bolstered by Japan. In June 1941 Germany invaded the Soviet Union. Then in December, Japan attacked a U.S. naval base, bringing the United States into World War II (1939–1945).

Nazi dictator Adolf Hitler, pictured in the late 1930s.

The War Turns

Throughout 1942 and 1943, Allied and Axis forces battled in North Africa, Italy, the Soviet Union, and the Pacific as the war went global. Italy surrendered in September 1943. In June 1944 Allied forces launched Operation Overlord to begin taking back Europe. Months of fighting followed before the Allies began to advance toward Germany, something that the Soviet Union had begun to do from the east. Crushed in a massive pincer movement, Nazi forces were defeated. Hitler committed suicide at the end of April 1945 as Germany's capital, Berlin, fell to the Allies.

The Atomic Bomb

In the Pacific the war had raged on. To end it, President Harry Truman authorized the use of the most terrible weapon ever invented—the atomic bomb—which obliterated the Japanese cities of Hiroshima and Nagasaki in August 1945. Japan finally surrendered. World War II was over.

The atomic "mushroom cloud" rises above Nagasaki, Japan.

A TERRIBLE TOLL

The cost of the war in human lives was staggering. Historians estimate that more than 21-25 million soldiers and up to 55 million civilians were killed. Around 6 million were Jews who were murdered by the Nazis during the Holocaust.

World War II on Land

Ground forces fought in every battleground of World War II, from western Europe to North Africa and from the Pacific Islands to Burma. This book looks at just a few of the brave units that fought on land during the war and describes some of their actions and equipment.

The battles of World War II were waged all over the world, in many different kinds of terrain.

THE BRITISH EXPEDITIONARY FORCE

FORMED: 1938	**STRENGTH:** 394,000
AREAS ACTIVE: France, Belgium	

On September 1, 1939, Germany invaded Poland. Later that month, Great Britain sent an army to help France and Belgium defend themselves against a Nazi invasion.

The BEF

Formed in 1938, the British Expeditionary Force (BEF) was created in response to the threat posed by Nazi aggression in Europe. Commanded by Field Marshal Lord Gort, its troops crossed the English Channel on September 9, 1939, taking up positions on the French/Belgian border. By March 1940 the BEF had been strengthened to more than 390,000 men.

Invasion and Retreat

German forces swept into France and Belgium on May 10, 1940. Over the next few weeks, troops of the BEF put up a brave fight, but were soon overwhelmed by the Nazi war machine. With his forces surrounded and supplies running low, Gort had no option but to order a retreat.

Soldiers of the British Expeditionary Force head to France on a troop ship in September 1939.

A German military parade along Paris' Champs Élysées

British soldiers train with SMLE Mk III rifles in eastern England in September 1939.

British Armada

By early June, much of the BEF had retreated to Dunkirk in northern France where, as the German air force, Luftwaffe, attacked, an armada of British ships evacuated 340,000 troops. Warships, ferries, and even fishing boats and little pleasure crafts all took part. Anyone with a boat who could find their way across the English Channel went to the rescue.

Rescue

As the German invasion continued, the remaining members of the BEF and other Allied forces retreated further down the coast. Still under constant attack, many more soldiers and civilians were rescued from ports such as Le Havre and Saint-Nazaire starting on June 15.

By late June 1940 more than 558,000 people had been evacuated—including 368,500 members of the BEF. On June 22 France officially surrendered to Nazi Germany.

- - - - - - - - - - - - - - - - - - -
SMLE RIFLE MK III
- - - - - - - - - - - - - - - - - - -

- **AMMUNITION** .303 caliber
- **MAGAZINE** 10 rounds
- **RANGE** 1,640 feet (500 meters)

The Short Magazine Lee-Enfield Mark III was the standard rifle used by British forces at the beginning of World War II. It fired .303-caliber bullets from a 10-round magazine. Its simple and reliable design meant that it saw active service well into the late 20th century.

More than 250,000 soldiers lined up to await rescue on the beach at Dunkirk in late May and early June 1940.

THE AFRIKA KORPS

FORMED: 1941	STRENGTH: 130,000
AREAS ACTIVE: North Africa	

The Afrika Korps was the Axis army that fought in North Africa from 1941 to 1943. Operating in searing desert heat and swirling sandstorms, the unit proved to be a tough opponent.

Why North Africa?

At the time of World War II, many European powers had colonies in Africa. Although Egypt had been an independent country since 1922, in effect it was controlled by Great Britain. Italy, ruled by Fascist dictator Benito Mussolini, had held Egypt's neighbor, Libya, as a colony since the 1910s.

On June 10, 1940, Italy, allied to Nazi Germany since 1936, declared war on France and Great Britain. Mussolini ordered his troops to invade Egypt. However, the Italian army was defeated by Allied forces in September and Mussolini had to ask Hitler for help.

An armored vehicle of the Afrika Korps, painted in sand camouflage.

War in the Desert

German military leaders formed the Afrika Korps in January 1941. One of Hitler's favorite generals, Erwin Rommel, was put in charge. In March Rommel went on the offensive, pushing the Allies back to the Libyan port of Tobruk before advancing into Egypt. To oppose the Afrika Korps, Allied leaders created the Eighth Army, which by August 1942 was commanded by General Bernard Montgomery.

The desert war seesawed back and forth throughout 1942 as both sides attempted to gain a decisive victory. After months of fighting, the Eighth Army won a major battle at El Alamein in Egypt in October 1942.

Advance to Victory

With the Eighth Army now advancing and the Afrika Korps in retreat, U.S. and other Allied forces launched Operation Torch in November 1942. By May 1943 the Allied forces had reached Tunisia, and the Afrika Korps was surrounded. Outgunned, it finally surrendered. More than 130,000 Axis soldiers became Allied prisoners of war.

ERWIN ROMMEL

Field Marshal Erwin Rommel (1891–1944) led an assault division during the invasion of France. He then commanded the Afrika Korps, before being recalled to Germany. Later, Rommel served in Italy and in France but was caught up in a plot to kill Hitler in 1944. Facing a trial that would have ended in his execution, Rommel chose to commit suicide instead.

Highly mobile, 88s were usually towed by a half-tracked vehicle, which also carried the gun's crew and ammunition.

- -

88-MM GUN

- -

- **AMMUNITION** 88-mm shells
- **RANGE** 9.3 miles (15 kilometers)

The highly mobile, long-range "88" was designed as an antiaircraft gun. However, it soon proved to be a very effective antitank weapon, firing up to 25 rounds per minute. Rommel deployed 88s extensively, drawing Allied tanks into ambushes, then using hidden 88s to pick them off.

Erwin Rommel (far left) pictured in his command vehicle in 1941.

THE FRENCH FOREIGN LEGION

FORMED:	STRENGTH:
1831	2,000 (13th Demi-Brigade)
AREAS ACTIVE: France, North Africa	

Formed in the 1800s to help protect French overseas territories, the French Foreign Legion was famed as an elite fighting unit well before the beginning of World War II.

Foreign Soldiers

The French Foreign Legion was unusual because it had always contained people who were not French citizens. By the late 1930s, up to 80 percent of the Legion's noncommissioned officers were German. With the rise of Hitler, Nazi propaganda targeted the Legion's German members. French commanders responded by sending sections of the Legion with a high German membership to French territories abroad.

Divided Loyalties

After the German invasion in 1940, France split into "Vichy" France, controlled by Nazi Germany, and "Free" France, led by General Charles de Gaulle. This was reflected within the French Foreign Legion. Some units, supporting Vichy France, fought against the Allies. Others, loyal to the Free French, fought with the Allies. The Legion's 1st Free French Brigade fought Axis forces at the Battle of Bir Hakeim in Libya between May 26 and June 21, 1942, helping to win the war in North Africa for the Allies.

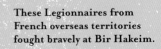

These Legionnaires from French overseas territories fought bravely at Bir Hakeim.

Wearing their distinctive high, round kepis, Legionnaires go into action.

Brilliant Brigade

The 13th Demi-Brigade became the most famous Legion unit of World War II. Deploying to the Middle East in 1941, the 13th Demi-Brigade fought with the Allies during the Battle of Damascus, in modern-day Syria. Here, Allied forces were opposed by Vichy-loyal Legionnaires so that units of the Legion were actually fighting each other.

After the Allied victory on July 21, many defeated Legionnaires chose to join the 13th Demi-Brigade, which became part of the Eighth Army opposing Axis forces in North Africa. Later in the war, the 13th Demi-Brigade became part of an expanded Legion which helped to free Rome and southern France from the Nazis.

BROWNING M2 HEAVY MACHINE GUN

- **AMMUNITION** .50 caliber
- **MAGAZINE** 450-600 rounds
- **RANGE** 5,900 feet (1,800 m)

The Browning M2 heavy machine gun was used by the Allies during World War II and is still in service with the French Foreign Legion today. The weapon was developed near the end of World War I to penetrate the steel armor then being introduced on vehicles and aircraft.

The Browning M2 heavy machine gun was developed for U.S. forces in 1918.

THE LONG-RANGE DESERT GROUP

FORMED:	STRENGTH:
1940	350
AREAS ACTIVE: North Africa	

During three years of challenging desert warfare, the Allies were able to deploy a secret weapon—the daring men of the Long-Range Desert Group (LRDG).

A specially modified vehicle of the LRDG crests a sand dune while on patrol.

Tough Missions

Formed in Egypt in 1940 by desert expert Major Ralph Bagnold, the LRDG undertook risky long-range patrols in order to gather information about enemy troop movements. They also went on dangerous missions such as destroying enemy fuel and ammunition depots behind enemy lines. The LRDG became part of General Bernard Montgomery's Eighth Army in 1942.

Vehicles and Weapons

To carry out their missions, the LRDG used trucks, usually rugged Fords or Chevrolets. These had specially adapted radiators and strengthened suspensions to allow them to operate in the desert. Anything that added weight, such as doors and roofs, was removed to allow the trucks to carry enough supplies and ammunition. LRDG trucks were armed with both medium machine guns and large-caliber antitank rifles.

Men of the LRDG return from a risky three-month mission in North Africa.

Tough Soldiers

At first, the men who served in the LRDG were mostly New Zealanders. As the LRDG expanded, British, Rhodesian (now Zimbabwe), and Indian soldiers joined the unit, which was divided up into patrols. Each patrol consisted of five or six vehicles carrying 15 to 18 men. A patrol always included a navigator, radio operator, medic, and a mechanic.

NAVIGATION

Finding the way in the desert was a challenge as accurate maps were rare. Vehicles carried a sun compass designed by Bagnold, as well as star tables that allowed navigators to find their way using the night sky. Of great importance were the radios the LRDG carried. As well as allowing patrols to communicate, they provided a check on Greenwich Mean Time—essential to enable LRDG navigators to plot their positions.

BERNARD MONTGOMERY

General (later Field Marshal) Bernard Montgomery (1887-1976) led the Eighth Army to victory at El Alamein in 1942. He went on to head invasions of Sicily and Italy, as well as the D-Day landings.

THE 7TH AUSTRALIAN INFANTRY DIVISION

FORMED:	STRENGTH:
1940	6,000
AREAS ACTIVE: Middle East, North Africa, Pacific	

The tough 7th Australian Infantry Division saw action in the Middle East and North Africa, before being posted to the island of New Guinea to help defend Australia from a Japanese invasion.

War in the Pacific

Japan entered World War II when it attacked the U.S. naval base at Pearl Harbor, Hawaii, on December 7, 1941. Throughout early 1942 the apparently unstoppable Japanese war machine steamrollered through the Pacific region.

By late July a Japanese invasion force reached the island of New Guinea. Landing on the northern coast at Buna, they moved south along the Kokoda Trail toward Port Moresby, from where an attack on Australia could easily be launched. The Japanese had to be stopped.

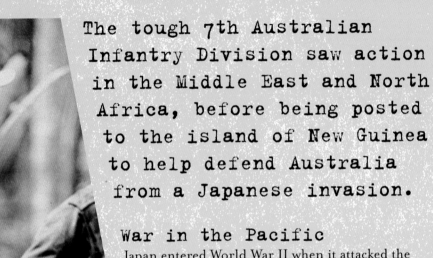

DIGGERS

Australian infantry were known as "Diggers"—a name that dated back to World War I. They were instantly recognizable with their distinctive slouch hats. During World War II many Diggers used the Australian-made Owen submachine gun. Invented in 1939, this weapon proved to be tough and reliable in combat.

Fighting the Advance

First on the scene were Australian troops of the 21st and 25th Brigades. These were soon strengthened by the battle-hardened men of the 7th Infantry Division, fresh from the desert war in North Africa.

Advancing from Port Moresby, the Australians met the enemy on July 23 but were pushed back. By the end of the month, the village of Kokoda was in Japanese hands. An attempt to recapture it on August 8 was unsuccessful, and soon the Australians had to retreat again—this time to within sight of Port Moresby.

On the Offensive

By October Japanese forces were running short of supplies. Taking advantage of this, the Australians went on the offensive, retaking Kokoda on November 2. By early 1943 the Japanese force had been pushed back as far as Buna, where further heavy fighting took place as Australian and U.S. forces attacked and destroyed the Japanese positions. Kokoda marked the furthest point south that Japanese forces were able to advance in the Pacific, and the campaign helped to save Australia.

This memorial in Papua New Guinea commemorates Japanese soldiers who died fighting on the Kokoda Trail.

KOKODA TRAIL

The Kokoda Trail was a narrow track that crossed New Guinea. Tanks and trucks were useless in the thick jungle. Most supplies had to be carried on foot. The climate was hot and humid, with high rainfall. The area was infested with insects carrying deadly tropical diseases such as malaria, dengue, and typhus, as well as with jungle parasites.

Australian troops haul a 25-pounder gun through the thick jungle mud.

THE SPECIAL AIR SERVICE

FORMED:		STRENGTH:
1941		2,000
AREAS ACTIVE: Mediterranean, North Africa, Western Europe		

The Special Air Service (SAS) was the brainchild of British officer Lieutenant-Colonel David Stirling. With its winged dagger insignia and "Who Dares Wins" motto, the SAS has become legendary for conducting dangerous secret missions.

Commandos training in Scotland in 1943

Beginnings

Stirling had been a member of the Commandos, the Royal Marine elite force founded in 1940. In 1941 he put forward the creation of a well-trained strike unit that could operate in small groups behind enemy lines, disrupting communications and destroying supply lines. The SAS was born.

Naming the SAS

The original name of the unit was "L Detachment, Special Air Service Brigade." This was designed to confuse the enemy by making them believe that the SAS was purely a paratrooper regiment. Members of the SAS did perform parachute drops, but were trained to reach their targets by land and sea as well.

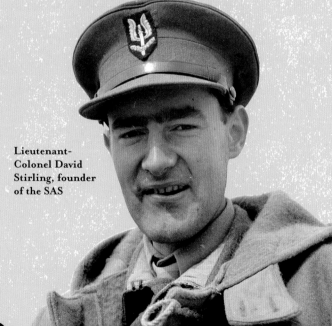

Lieutenant-Colonel David Stirling, founder of the SAS

Into Action

The SAS deployed to North Africa with five officers and 60 other ranks. However, its first mission in November 1941 was a disaster—22 SAS men were killed or captured. Given a second chance, the unit performed much better. The SAS team attacked three Libyan airfields, destroying 60 enemy planes.

In June 1942 the SAS raided airfields on the German-occupied island of Crete. It also continued to operate in North Africa, with Stirling leading his men in attacks that destroyed many key targets. By the end of 1942, the SAS had grown to include four British squadrons, one Free French squadron, one Greek squadron, and a boat section.

STIRLING CAPTURED

In 1943 Stirling was captured by the Italians in Tunisia. He spent the rest of the war as a prisoner and, after many escape attempts, found himself in the infamous Colditz Castle prison. Stirling was replaced as leader by Lieutenant-Colonel Robert "Paddy" Mayne. Under Mayne's leadership the SAS continued to strike at Axis forces in North Africa and Italy and, later, worked with the French Resistance.

STEN GUN

- **AMMUNITION** 9- x 19-mm parabellum cartridge
- **MAGAZINE** 32 rounds
- **RANGE** 328 feet (100 m)

The Sten gun was a submachine gun used by British forces during the war. Although sometimes unreliable and prone to jamming, the Sten's small size and light weight made it ideal for secret missions. The Sten gun could also fire up to 500 rounds per minute.

Sten Mk 2 submachine gun

Members of No.2 SAS carry a heavy machine gun and its ammunition up a mountain path during a mission to help Italian guerrilla fighters battle Nazi forces in 1943–44.

SOVIET 62ND ARMY

FORMED:	STRENGTH:
1942	120,000
AREAS ACTIVE: Eastern Front	

In June 1941 Hitler's forces invaded the Soviet Union in Operation Barbarossa. More than 4 million Axis troops swept eastward in the largest land invasion in history.

Why the Soviet Union?

Germany's aim was to populate the western Soviet Union with German-speaking people. This key Nazi policy was to result in some of the most extreme fighting of World War II, as the Soviets desperately defended their homeland.

Advance to Stalingrad

By August 1942 the German 6th Army, commanded by General Friedrich Paulus, as well as the 4th Panzer Army, had reached the key Soviet city of Stalingrad. It was vital to the Soviet war effort that Stalingrad should not fall. Located on the Volga River, the city contained steelworks as well as arms, tank, and chemical factories. The 62nd Army, created to defend the city, was formed by combining Red Army units in the area. Tough and resourceful, General Vasily Chuikov was put in charge.

Soviet troops fight building-to-building during the battle for Stalingrad.

CHUIKOV

Vasily Ivanovich Chuikov (1900–82) first became a soldier during the 1917 Russian civil war. After Stalingrad, Chuikov was made Marshal of the Soviet Union in 1955 and became Chief of Soviet Armed Forces in 1960.

Fighting Clever

The troops of the 62nd Army forced the Germans to fight for every building and inch of ground, often many times over. Sometimes the German attackers, having taken a day to clear a street of defenders, would find that by the next day the Soviets had used a hidden network of tunnels to reoccupy their earlier positions. Skilled Soviet snipers wearing winter camouflage gear killed hundreds of German soldiers.

Soviet soldiers advance against Paulus'
6th Army through the rubble of
Stalingrad in November 1942.

The End

By late autumn 1942 Axis forces had captured parts of the tank factory, the arms factory, and the steelworks. They had pushed their Soviet opponents back to narrow zones along the banks of the Volga River, so that reinforcements had to be ferried across the river, vulnerable to aerial attacks.

But help was at hand for the 62nd Army. On November 19 Chuikov's commander, General Georgi Zhukov, ordered a massive counterattack with reinforcements he had been assembling nearby. The 6th Army was cut off and surrounded. Hitler ordered the attackers to be resupplied by air, but to no avail. By February 1943 the Axis forces had run out of food and ammunition. The German 6th Army surrendered, and more than 100,000 Axis soldiers were taken prisoner. The battle for Stalingrad had cost more than 750,000 lives.

Exhausted German prisoners captured at Stalingrad, 1943

WAFFEN-SS PANZER DIVISIONS

	FORMED: 1939-1943	STRENGTH: Between 15,000- 20,000 per unit
	AREAS ACTIVE: Europe, Balkans, Eastern Front	

The Waffen-SS was one of the most feared parts of the Nazi war machine. Responsible to Hitler's deputy, Heinrich Himmler, Waffen-SS troops fought throughout Europe.

Who Were They?

Elite Waffen-SS assault troops were armed with the very best weapons and equipment. At first, membership of Waffen-SS units was limited to Germans. Later, men from Nazi-occupied countries were allowed to join. Waffen-SS soldiers took an oath of loyalty to Adolf Hitler and the Nazis, promising to fight to the death for the Nazi cause.

Here are some of the most infamous Waffen-SS units:

2nd SS Panzer Division
Das Reich (The Empire)

This formidable force fought in the invasion of France, Belgium, and the Netherlands in 1940, and in the Balkans during 1941. Das Reich then took part in Germany's invasion of the Soviet Union. Later in the war, the unit fought in Normandy and Belgium before being sent east once more to try to stop Soviet forces from reaching the Hungarian capital, Budapest, in December 1944.

WAFFEN-SS

EINTRITT NACH VOLLENDETEM 17. LEBENSJAHR

A Nazi Waffen-SS recruiting poster

3rd SS Panzer Division Totenkopf (Death's Head)

Named for its death's-head badge, this unit was first formed from soldiers who acted as guards for brutal

A Waffen-SS member's Totenkopf ring

Nazi concentration camps. After attacking France, the Netherlands, and Belgium in 1940, the force was transferred to the Eastern Front, where it fought at Leningrad, Kursk, and later in Poland and Hungary.

12th SS Panzer Division Hitler Jugend (Hitler Youth)

This unit was formed in 1943. It was mainly made up of teenage soldiers who had been members of the Hitler Youth, the Nazi Party's organization for young people. The 12th Panzer Division fought with fanatical courage in France and Belgium in 1944, and on the Eastern Front right at the end of the war in 1945.

PANZER IV TANK

- **ARMAMENT** 1- x 75-mm cannon; 2- x 7.92-mm machine guns
- **RANGE** 124 miles (200 km)

The most widely manufactured German tank of World War II, the Panzer IV saw action with many units, including Waffen-SS Panzer divisions. Armed with a cannon and two machine guns, the Panzer IV had 3-inch (80-mm) thick armor and could travel up to 26 miles (42 km) per hour.

Members of the Hitler Youth on parade

1ST SPECIAL SERVICE FORCE

	FORMED: 1942	**STRENGTH:** 1,800
USA CANADA	**AREAS ACTIVE:** Western Europe, Mediterranean	

By 1942 U.S. troops and equipment were beginning to cross the Atlantic to reinforce the Allied war effort. After the defeat of Axis forces in North Africa, the Allies invaded Sicily and then Italy. The elite U.S./Canadian 1st Special Service Force was deployed to help with special operations.

Tough Recruits

The 1st Special Service Force (SSF) was formed in autumn 1942. Many of the recruits were tough backwoodsmen who possessed excellent hunting, tracking, and survival skills. After some of its early deployments were aborted, the 1st SSF was finally sent to Italy, where Allied forces were attempting to push north and capture the Italian capital, Rome.

Daring Ops

The men of the 1st SSF went into action in December 1943 when they climbed a mountain near Cassino under cover of night to attack a key German position. The unit took heavy casualties but succeeded in capturing the stronghold. The 1st SSF conducted further operations in the Italian hills before being reassigned to Anzio in February 1944. Here, U.S. and British forces made amphibious landings in an attempt to speed up the Allied push toward Rome.

U.S. troops fill a landing craft from a support ship as they prepare to assault the beach at Anzio, Italy.

The Road to Rome

Following the breakout of Allied forces from Anzio, the men of the 1st SSF attacked and held key bridges on the road to Rome, before spearheading the Allied army that finally freed the Italian capital on June 5, 1944. But there was to be no rest for the men—they were then immediately sent to southern France as part of Operation Dragoon, the Allied advance through the mountains bordering Italy.

Disbanded

By December 1944 the 1st SSF had suffered heavy casualties, but had killed or wounded more than 12,000 of the enemy. Depleted in strength and with its remaining men exhausted, Allied commanders disbanded the unit. But the toughness and courage displayed by the men of the 1st SSF laid the foundations for the many Special Ops units that are part of the world's armed forces today.

IN THE DARK

Operations under the cover of darkness were often part of the exploits of the 1st SSF. To stay hidden, its troops would apply boot polish to their faces and creep up noiselessly on enemy soldiers.

M1 BAZOOKA

- **AMMUNITION** M6 RPG (Rocket-Propelled Grenade)
- **WEIGHT** 13 pounds (6 kg) (unloaded)
- **RANGE** 98-328 feet (30-100 m)

The M1 Bazooka was a portable U.S. antitank weapon. Firing an explosive rocket-propelled grenade capable of punching through thick steel armor, Bazookas took out German tanks such as the Panzer IV.

U.S. 1ST INFANTRY DIVISION

FORMED:	STRENGTH:
1917	15,500

AREAS ACTIVE:	
Mediterranean, Western Europe, North Africa	

On June 6, 1944, Operation Overlord began when Allied troops landed in northern France to begin the liberation of Europe from Nazi forces. The U.S. 1st Infantry Division was in the thick of the fighting.

History

The U.S. 1st Infantry Division was formed in 1917 when the United States joined World War I. During World War II, troops of the 1st Infantry Division participated in Operation Torch. They then fought in Sicily, capturing Troina on July 29, 1943. After Sicily the unit was ordered to Great Britain to regroup and prepare for its toughest challenge yet.

D-Day

Allied leaders had been planning Operation Overlord, or "D-Day," since 1943. The landings that took place in June 1944 were part of the biggest seaborne assault in history. More than 10,000 aircraft and 4,000 ships took part, together with 156,000 Allied troops. Allied leaders chose five Normandy beaches for the assaults, code-named Omaha, Utah, Juno, Sword, and Gold.

U.S. troops fill a landing craft as they head toward the Normandy beaches on June 6, 1944.

Bloody Omaha

As they landed on Omaha Beach, the men of the U.S. 1st Infantry Division met with fierce resistance. Soldiers who made it onto the beach were pinned down by enemy fire. Officers organized their men into assault groups and broke through enemy defenses. By the evening of June 6 the 1st Infantry Division was still in action. Many combat teams had lost up to 30 percent of their men, but they had fought their way about 1.6 miles (2.5 km) inland.

What Happened Next

In the months that followed, the 1st Infantry Division was involved in vicious fighting before joining the Allied breakout. Advancing eastward in a continuous assault, in October they captured Aachen—the first German city to fall to the Allies. After helping to drive back the German winter offensive in the Ardennes Forest—the so-called Battle of the Bulge—in late 1944 and early 1945, the 1st Infantry Division eventually crossed the Rhine River into Germany and pushed onward as far as Czechoslovakia (now divided into the Czech Republic and Slovakia). Troops of the 1st Division remained in Germany as part of the occupying Allied forces until the 1950s.

M1 CARBINE

- **AMMUNITION** .30-caliber
- **MAGAZINE** 15 rounds
- **RANGE** 886 feet (270 m)

Issued to infantry officers, paratroopers, and other frontline U.S. soldiers during World War II, the M1 carbine was lightweight and reliable. More than 6 million M1s were produced, making it the most produced U.S. military small arm during the war.

The M1 carbine packed a big punch for its small size and light weight.

U.S. soldiers advance across open ground during the Battle of the Bulge in December 1944.

U.S. RANGERS

	FORMED: 1941	STRENGTH: 3,500
	AREAS ACTIVE: North Africa, Western Europe, Pacific	

The U.S. Army had included "ranger" battalions since the 1780s. The term originally referred to light infantry soldiers who combined both European and Native American styles of warfare.

Rangers Reborn

In 1942 U.S. Major General Lucian Truscott proposed a new special operations/airborne force and the 1st Ranger Battalion was created. The first Rangers fought alongside British and Canadian commandos in the disastrous Dieppe Raid of August 1942. Here, a combined invasion force attempted a seaborne landing on the French coast but were driven back by the German defenders, who inflicted heavy casualties.

Although Dieppe was a failure, it demonstrated to the Allies that no assault on the French coast could be made without massive air and naval support.

Mediterranean

In 1943 the 1st, 3rd, and 4th Ranger Battalions fought in North Africa and Italy. But disaster struck when the Rangers, who were operating at night behind German lines in an effort to capture the Italian town of Cisterna, were ambushed by the enemy. Of the 767 men in the three battalions, 761 were killed or captured.

U.S. Rangers and French troops return from the failed raid on Dieppe.

U.S. troops and equipment pour onto Omaha Beach on D-Day, June 6, 1944.

D-Day

Both the 2nd and 5th Ranger Battalions took part in D-Day. Landing ahead of the main U.S. forces, the 2nd Rangers were tasked with climbing 100-foot (30-m) cliffs to find and destroy five heavy guns. Under constant fire, the Rangers scaled the cliffs but found no guns, which had been moved. However, after following tracks in the mud, the unit discovered the weapons and destroyed them. The Rangers then held the main road for two days before other Allied forces relieved them.

Freed U.S. soldiers from the Cabanatuan POW camp

RANGERS IN THE PACIFIC

Rangers operated in the Pacific too. On January 30, 1945, the 6th Ranger Battalion made a daring secret raid on a Japanese prisoner-of-war (POW) camp at Cabanatuan in the Philippines. Working with local Filipino guerrillas and using air support to distract the Japanese, the men of the 6th Rangers trekked deep behind enemy lines to attack the camp. They set free 552 prisoners. More than 500 Japanese soldiers were killed in the assault on the camp, which lasted just 35 minutes. The Rangers' casualties were just two killed and four wounded.

Rangers on their way to Normandy.

THE CHINDITS

	FORMED: 1942	STRENGTH: 3,000-9,000
	AREAS ACTIVE: Burma (now Myanmar)	

In 1942 the Imperial Japanese Army invaded and occupied Burma. This act directly threatened nearby India, which at the time was governed by Great Britain.

Chindits move along a jungle trail in Burma in January 1944. Mules were essential for carrying supplies.

A New Strike Force

Brigadier Orde Wingate commanded British units in Africa early in the war. Transferring to Burma, he created a strike force that could operate on foot deep behind enemy lines. The new unit was named the "Chindits" after the Chinthay, a mythical Burmese dragon. Chindit recruits trained in India, learning jungle warfare tactics. They deployed to Burma in eight columns armed with machine guns, antitank rifles, and light antiaircraft guns.

First Operations

On February 8, 1943, the Chindits began operations by blowing up railway tracks to disrupt Japanese supply lines. Wingate's troops hacked their way through dense jungle to reach their targets. After three months of vicious fighting, Wingate ordered a withdrawal. Of the 3,000 men who marched into Burma, 818 had been killed, taken prisoner, or died of disease. These first missions, although costly, boosted Allied morale as they demonstrated that Japanese forces—previously thought unbeatable—could be defeated.

With bayonets fixed, Chindits advance into the thick jungle in Burma.

Second Phase

In the second phase of Chindit operations, airborne troops built fortified jungle bases from which columns of men could attack the enemy. In February 1944 transport aircraft flew in 9,000 men and bases were established, but nonstop Japanese attacks meant that the Chindits were engaged in continuous hand-to-hand fighting in terrible conditions.

New Commander, New Tactics

After Wingate was killed in a plane crash in 1944, new commander Brigadier Walter "Joe" Lentaigne moved the force north where, from new bases, it continued to disrupt enemy supply lines. However, by August 1944, the men of the Chindits were exhausted and had taken heavy casualties—1,396 killed and 2,434 wounded. The Chindits were withdrawn from Burma, but not before their efforts had caused huge disruptions to enemy forces.

Glossary

Allied forces (AL-lyd FORSS-uhs)—the military forces of Great Britain, its empire and dominions, France and, after 1941, the Soviet Union and the United States

amphibious (am-FI-bee-uhs)—relating to an attack where vehicles and troops are landed from the sea

armistice (ARM-iss-tiss)—an agreement between warring sides to stop fighting while a settlement is reached

Axis powers (AK-siss POU-urz)—the military forces of Nazi Germany, Italy, Japan, and some other countries

bayonet (BAY-uh-net)—a large blade that can be fixed to the end of a rifle for close-quarter fighting

brigade (bri-GAYD)—a large military unit consisting of hundreds of soldiers

caliber (KA-luh-buhr)—the width of the inside of a gun's barrel

casualty (KAZH-oo-uhl-tee)—a person killed, wounded, or missing in a battle or in a war

colony (KAH-luh-nee)—territory that is ruled by another country far away

commando (kuh-MAN-doh)—an elite soldier trained to undertake particularly dangerous or difficult missions

death's head (DETHS HED)—a symbol that looks like a skull and crossbones

deploy (di-PLOY)—to move troops or equipment into action

dictator (DIK-tay-tuhr)—a leader who wields supreme power to control a country and its people

dominions (duh-MIN-yuhnz)—countries that in the past were part of the British Empire, but had their own government

empire (EM-pire)—a group of countries under the control of a single government or ruler

evacuate (i-VA-kyuh-wayt)—to remove to safety in an emergency

Fascist (FASH-ist)—a political movement of the 1930s where a country unites as a disciplined force behind a nationalistic, all-powerful leader

guerrilla (guh-RIL-ah)—paramilitary soldier who fights an enemy using unconventional means

Holocaust (HOL-uh-kost)—the mass murder of millions of Jews, as well as gypsies, the disabled, homosexuals, and political and religious leaders during World War II

landing craft (LAND-ing KRAFT)—a flat-bottomed vessel designed to deliver soldiers and vehicles onto a beach

loyalty (LOI-uhl-tee)—a strong love for a country, person, or cause

magazine (MAG-uh-zeen)—the part of a gun containing the bullets

Nazi (NOT-see)—a member of Adolf Hitler's National Socialist Party

Timeline

1939

September 1 Nazi Germany invades Poland; World War II begins

September 3 Great Britain and France declare war on Germany

September BEF sails for France

1940

April Nazi Germany invades Denmark and Norway

May 10 Nazi Germany invades the Netherlands, Belgium, and France

May 26 The Allied evacuation at Dunkirk, known as Operation Dynamo, begins

June 11 Italy joins the war on the Axis side

June 22 France signs an armistice with Nazi Germany

July 10–October 31 The Battle of Britain—Great Britain's Royal Air Force defeats Nazi Luftwaffe

September 1940–May 1941 Nazi "Blitz" (aerial bombing campaign) on Great Britain

December Great Britain defeats Italian forces in North Africa

1941

February Hitler sends Rommel's Afrika Korps to North Africa

April Italy and Germany invade Yugoslavia and Greece

June 22 Nazis invade Soviet Union

December 7 Japanese attack Pearl Harbor, Hawaii; the United States enters war on Allied side

December 25 Japanese capture Hong Kong

noncommissioned officer (non-kuh-MISH-uhnd OF-uh-sur)—a soldier, such as a sergeant, who commands a small group of military personnel

obliterate (uh-BLIT-uh-rate)—to destroy or wipe out utterly

offensive (uh-FEN-siv)—a planned military attack, often using large forces

paratrooper (PAIR-uh-troop-ur)—a soldier who deploys from an aircraft by parachute

patrol (puh-TROHL)—a small group of soldiers sent out to get information about the enemy

pincer movement (PIN-sur MOOV-muhnt)—a military strategy designed to encircle and trap enemy forces

prisoner of war (PRIZ-uhn-ur UHV WAR)—a soldier taken captive and held by enemy forces during a war

propaganda (prop-ah-GAN-da)—when a government spreads information, often incorrect, in order to make people think or behave a certain way

sniper (SNY-pur)—a soldier who is an expert shot and is trained to shoot and kill the enemy one by one

submachine gun (suhb-muh-SHEEN GUHN)—a light, easily carried machine gun

treaty (TREE-tee)—an official agreement between nations, such as that which ends a war

Read More

Chandler, Matt. *Behind Enemy Lines: The Escape of Robert Grimes with the Comet Line.* Great Escapes of World War II. North Mankato, Minn.: Capstone Press, 2017.

Doeden, Matt. *Weapons of World War II.* Weapons of War. North Mankato, Minn.: Capstone Press, 2018.

Murray, Laura K. *World War II Technology.* War Technology. Minneapolis: Abdo Publishing, 2018.

Williams, Brian. *World War II.* DK Findout! New York: DK Publishing, 2017.

Yomtov, Nel. *Tunneling to Freedom: The Great Escape from Stalag Luft III.* Great Escapes of World War II. North Mankato, Minn.: Capstone Press, 2017.

Internet Sites

The International Museum of World War II
https://museumofworldwarii.org

The National World War II Museum: New Orleans
https://www.nationalww2museum.org

Smithsonian National Air and Space Museum: World War II
https://airandspace.si.edu/topics/world-war-ii

1942

February 15 Japanese capture Singapore and take 60,000 Allied prisoners

May Battle of Bir Hakeim

June 4–7 U.S. Navy defeats Japanese at key Battle of Midway

July–November Australian forces battle with Japan on the Kokoda Trail in New Guinea

August Montgomery takes over Allied Eighth Army in North Africa

November 11 Allies defeat Afrika Korps at El Alamein

November The Battle of Stalingrad begins

November 8 Operation Torch begins—U.S. troops land in North Africa; the Allies begin to close in on Axis forces

1943

February 2 Soviet forces defeat Nazi forces at Stalingrad

May 13 Axis forces surrender in North Africa; 275,000 taken prisoner

July 9 Allies invade Sicily

September 3 Allied forces invade Italy at Salerno

September 8 Italy surrenders; Nazi Germany now opposes Allied advance through Italy

1944

January 22 Allied forces land at Anzio, Italy

January–May key Battle of Monte Cassino in Italy

June 5 Rome liberated

June 6 D-Day—Allied armies invade Normandy to begin freeing Europe from Nazi forces

August 25 Paris liberated

December 16 Battle of the Bulge begins—Nazi Germany launches its final, unsuccessful offensive in the Ardennes region of France

1945

March 23 Allied forces cross the Rhine River into Germany

April 1 Battle of Okinawa—the armed forces of the United States and Japan do battle in the Pacific

April/May Soviet forces close in on Berlin; Hitler commits suicide on April 30 as the German capital falls

May 7 Nazi forces surrender

May 8 VE (Victory in Europe) Day—the war in Europe ends

August 6, August 9 United States drops atomic bombs on Hiroshima and Nagasaki in Japan

August 15 Japan surrenders; VJ (Victory over Japan) Day—the war in the Pacific ends

Index